What Can You Measure With a Lollipop?

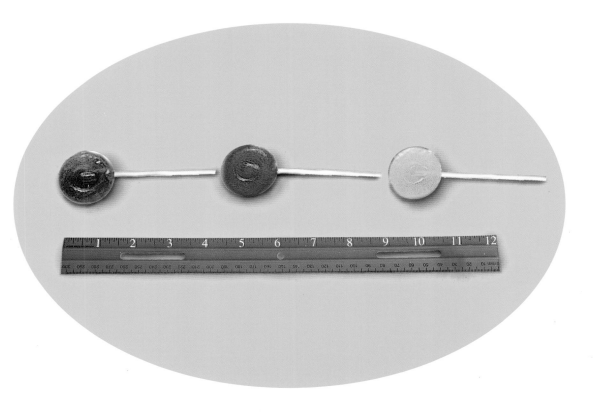

by Margie Burton, Cathy French, and Tammy Jones

We can measure with a lot
of things.

We can use a
tape measure.

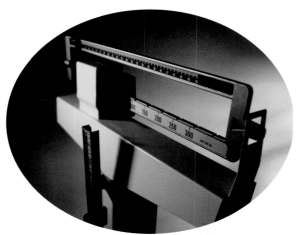

We can use
a scale.

We can use a ruler.

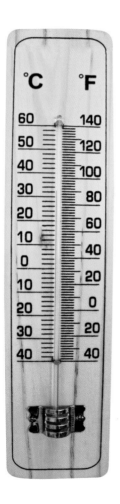

We can use
a thermometer.

Our teacher told
us to think of
something new
to measure with.

5

My friend said we should use lollipops to measure with. We were going to have fun.

You can measure a lot
of things with lollipops!

We measured one of the desks.

The desk was about 5 lollipops long

We measured our teacher's desk.
It was very long.

His desk was 11 lollipops long.

We measured a word on the chalkboard.

The word was 1 lollipop long.

We measured one of our books, too.

The book was over 2 lollipops long.

We measured the hall.
The hall was very wide.

Look at all the lollipops!
The hall was 16 lollipops wide.

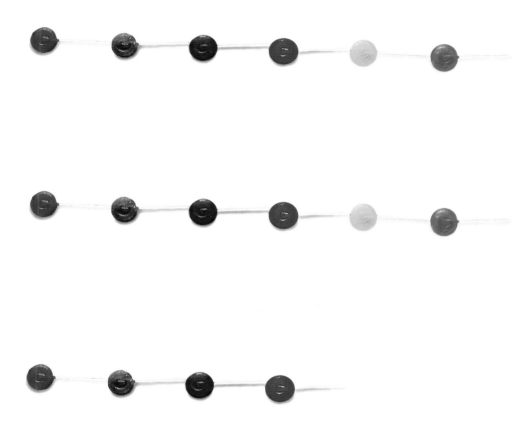

We measured our class pets.
Our goldfish was not very long.

Our gerbil was not very long.

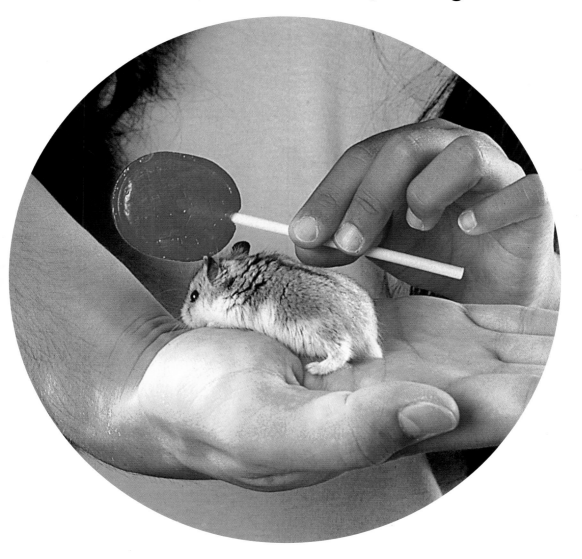

Our class pets were not even one lollipop long.

It was fun to measure with lollipops

	What did we measure?	
1.		student's desk
2.		teacher's desk
3.	pop	word "pop"
4.		book
5.		hall
6.		goldfish
7.		gerbil